— THE —
CALL

(MY JOURNEY WITH CHRIST)

REJOICE
ESI HLOVOR

THE CALL: MY JOURNEY WITH CHRIST

ISBNS:
978-1-952744-19-8(PB)
978-1-952744-24-2 (EB)
978-1-952744-23-5 (HC)

Published By:
Eleviv Publishing Group
Centerville, OH 45458
elevivpublishing.com
info@elevivpublishing.com
1-937-907-5001

Published in the United States of America

10 9 8 7 6 5 4 3 2

APPRECIATION

I am grateful to God Almighty for the inspiration He provided throughout the course of writing this book. Truly, the wisdom of God surpasses the understanding of man, and what we think we know about God only scratches the surface of who He really is.

God never leaves His servant alone when He sends them on a journey. He gives them all they need to succeed in any given assignment. So far, this has been my story, and I am grateful to God for the spiritual and physical backups He made available in a most extraordinary way. I also thank Him for releasing His Holy Spirit of truth that directs me in all I do.

I appreciate God for the gift of mentors and spiritual directors. Most significantly, for sending some amazing and spirit-filled mentors my way– Apostle Belema Abili and Apostle Paul Gidi Gasu. These two have constantly given me the support and encouragement that have helped me immensely in my online ministry. I also thank God for the Lioness Group, a group comprising of amazing women of God like Prophetess Juliet Dean, Ashley Ngocha, and other notable people of God, for being a strong support system for me in those turbulent days.

I appreciate the support of my mother, Evangelist Fafa Hlovor, and my entire family for their undying love, support, and understanding throughout the birthing process of this book. They have really shown me what a true family should be.

I want to thank Fidelia Esharefasa, who took out time to proofread and edit this book despite her busy schedule. I thank Justin Onyema, who has also been of immense help in many ways.

To my Facebook followers, I appreciate the fact that you believe in me and, most importantly, that you recognize the power of God working in and through me. May God bless you abundantly.

TABLE OF CONTENT

CHAPTER SEVEN:

CHAPTER EIGHT:

Final note

Words of knowledge

Engage yourself in this series of prayer points, using the appropriate powerful scriptures

Conclusion

About the author

Notes

INTRODUCTION

For several months, after the birth of Rejoice E. Ministries on social media, it laid heavily in my Spirit to write this book to tell the world of the wonders that God has done for and through me since I answered His call. However, as with my hesitancy before finally answering God's call, I equally procrastinated in writing this book until now.

My name is Rejoice Esi Hlovor, a servant and mouthpiece of God. Upon answering the call of God in July 2020, He named me a Prophetess. I am from the Volta region of Ghana, currently living and working in Dublin, Ireland. I am a mother of three adorable children, and I work as a Care Support Personnel.

I am filled with so much joy because what started as a mere thought has finally come to reality in the birthing of this book. Right from the day I accepted the call of God to preach salvation and deliverance to millions of people on Facebook, my life has equally seen dramatic changes for the better. Since then, the urge to write this book had been laid heavily in my Spirit, which finally came to life by the special grace of God Almighty.

Being in the Ministry of Salvation and Deliverance

is very tough because you directly oppose the Kingdom of darkness. However, God has been with me all the way, fighting every battle that the devil continually wages against me because He had promised me from the onset that, *"I will never leave you, nor forsake you." Hebrews 13:5.*

This book is written to recount all that I have been through thus far as a minister, as well as what God has done for me. I know someone out there may have doubted if God can really make them His vessel. My story is meant to inspire you and to let you know that God truly can use you. If He can use me to do great things, then He can use you to do even greater things; all you have to do is believe in Him.

There are also valuable lessons embedded in this book that will, without a doubt, open your mind and heart to a complete understanding of what you need to do to succeed in the assignment that God sends you to accomplish. It is my earnest prayer and hope that you will receive fresh insight as you read through the contents of this book.

God bless you

CHAPTER ONE

ANSWERING THE CALL

"For I am not ashamed of the gospel of Christ: for it is the power of God unto salvation to everyone that believeth; to the Jew first and also to the Greek."
Romans 1:16 (KJV)

Being a true Christian is a most challenging lifestyle. No wonder we have many lukewarm Christians all over the world who are neither cold nor hot. I know this because I am speaking from experience. Being a lukewarm Christian will pave the way for distractions, therefore worship God with all your heart.

To be honest, this journey in Christ has not been an easy one. There are times when I face situations that weigh me down and drain my Spirit. However, in these times, I cling to His words in the Book of 2 Corinthians 12:9 (NIV): *"But he said to me, "My grace is sufficient for you, for my power is made perfect in weakness." Therefore I will boast all the more gladly about my weaknesses, so THAT Christ's power may rest on me." (NIV)*

These words alone gave me renewed strength anytime I felt weak, especially in my Spirit. I am a Born-

Again Christian, and since I gave my life to Christ and clung to His words, I have witnessed remarkable changes in my life and in the lives of all who come in contact with me.

While growing up, preaching the gospel of Christ was not part of my life's goals. I studied Marketing in Customer Service at the Ibat College Dublin and obtained a Certificate in Science Bio-Pharmaceutical Processing from IT Sligo University, both in Ireland.

So, there was nothing like Theology in my plans. However, God has a way of stirring us back on the right path towards the purpose He created us to fulfill. Remember His words to Jeremiah in the Book of *Jeremiah 1:5: "Before I formed you in the womb I knew you, before you were born I set you apart; I appointed you as a prophet to the nations."*

God repeatedly gave me signs that showed me He wanted me to be His mouthpiece — His prophetess. However, every time the signs came, I kept ignoring them. I could not imagine myself being responsible for the lives of millions of people — people whose lives my message would affect. I did not even know whether they would listen to me or not. Most importantly, I did not believe in my ability to become the mouthpiece of God. Thus, I ignored his call repeatedly, just as Jonah ignored God's instruction to preach to the people of Nineveh. In life, it is better to listen to God and follow his instructions because his plans for us are simply the best for our lives. He clearly stated this in *Jeremiah 29:11: For I know the plans I have for you," declares the Lord, "plans to prosper you and not to harm you, plans to give you hope and a future." (NIV)*

Failure to listen to and follow God's instructions always ends in disaster. Yes, as humans, we might have our own plans, but trust me, the plan of God shall always prevail (Proverbs 19:21). In everything, I am eternally grateful to Almighty God that I finally took heed and allowed him to use me.

I recall vividly when this happened. It was on a quiet night on July 4, 2020, while I was asleep. In my dream, God told me that He wanted me to preach on social media - Facebook, to be precise. He said in the exact words, "Prophetess Rejoice, accept your call! I am the salt of the earth!" He came in the form of Apostle Belema Abili. On the second day in my dream, God gave me a prayer cloth representing the power to pray like never before. I was strengthened for my journey and was ready to take the message of Christ to the millions of people who daily made use of Facebook. That was how Rejoice E. Ministries was birthed on Facebook. Personally, I had no intention of becoming a prophetess of God, as I said earlier. I wanted to be a nurse and help the sick and ailing. That was what I believed God's purpose for my life was. However, when He called me, here reminded me of the great commission in the gospel of Mark 16:15: *He said to them, "Go into all the world and preach the gospel to all creation" (NIV)*

In the end, there is no greater calling than to serve God. There is no greater contribution than to help the weak and the needy. There is no greater satisfaction than to have done it well– as God intended. Why am I telling you this story? I know you may be going through a dilemma – similar or different– in your life. Perhaps, God has called you to take up a role that you find challenging, or He may want you to leave where you are to go where He wants you to be. You know exactly what the signs He constantly gives you say. I am here to tell you not to be afraid. Do not let fear, especially of the unknown, cripple you. Remember he says in 2 Corinthians 12:9, that His grace is enough for you. In addition, He said in Jeremiah 29:11, that His thoughts towards you are those of good, to bring you to an expected end.

God is not one to leave his children halfway; He is not a man to lie (Numbers 23:19). For whatever journey He calls us to, He has fully prepared what we would need. He sees the end from the beginning, and His presence never departs from us. If you are reading this, I want you to know that God has your best interests at heart. Place your trust entirely in Him, and take that first step in faith, believing that He is with you every step of the way.

A PRAYER FOR YOU

Say this prayer: Lord Jesus, I believe in the plans you have for me. I surrender my fears and anxieties to you, and I trust you will guide me to fulfill the purpose you created me for. Amen.

CHAPTER TWO

GOD JUSTIFIES THE CALLED

"And those He predestined, He also called; those He called, He also justified; those He justified, He also glorified."
ROMANS 8:30 (NIV)

Answering God's call in mid-2020 was the best decision I had ever made so far. Since I decided to work for Him, He has taken my cares and burdens upon Himself and has done miraculous deeds; not only in my life but also in the lives of all those I minister to. My spiritual eyes have been opened to see what ordinary eyes cannot see.

God continues to reveal Himself to me in my dreams and during my prayer times. On one occasion, during my private prayer session, God appeared to me in a vision. In the vision, He handed to me three items that would help move my ministry. The first item was a sword -to help me fight all the battles I might encounter in ministry.

The next items were three pairs of shoes representing God the Father, God the Son, and God the Holy Spirit of comfort. This was the explanation I was given in the vision. After I was given the three pairs of shoes, I saw a man of God anoint each of my feet with anointing oil before putting the shoes on my feet. The final item that I received was a hat full of feathers. God told me the hat was a sign to show the preparation for the victory waiting for me upon successfully completing my race here on earth.

With these, I was given the assurance that God was with me in my online evangelism-The physical and spiritual strength (the sword) to fight every battle that may come my way in ministry, the indwelling presence of the Godhead, and the outpouring of the Holy Spirit (the three pairs of shoes) to comfort me and direct me on ministry growth, and lastly the assurance that I would receive the crown of glory (the hat full of feathers) if I ran my race to the finish line. *Romans 8:30 (NIV),* quoted earlier, puts this beautifully: *"And those He predestined, He also called; those He called, He also justified; those He justified, He also glorified."*

All these go on to show that there is no way God would send you on a journey without properly equipping you with the tools you would need to complete it successfully. I have clearly seen Him do this in my life and ministry, proving that His hands guide my ministry.

I am by no means better than anyone. However, this is an assignment that He has entrusted in my care - a burden that He laid heavily on my heart - and I would not have known peace if I did not harken to His call.

Since I started ministering for God, He has not disappointed me, and He never will. The words I speak by His direction have brought healing and salvation to many. Souls have been won back to Christ, the faith of many have been strengthened and restored, and the Gospel of Christ has been accepted by many - all through the power of God at work in me.

Many of us doubt what great things God can use us to achieve. We begin to look at how unworthy we are to utter His holy name. We let our past lives torment us into thinking that God has no use for us. Allow me to tell you this day that God is interested in you. Yes, you! and He wants you to accept His call, and He will do the rest. Romans 8:30 shows us that God justifies the 'called'. He does not call the justified. And if we were to be honest, there would be no just person on earth without God's justification. Therefore, why do you keep doubting and condemning yourself when God has not? Allow Him to use you today, and your life will never be the same.

A PRAYER FOR YOU

Say this prayer: Righteous father, I give myself to you this day. Open my spiritual eyes to see your plans for me and my mind to understand your will for my life. Help me realize that I am your vessel to be used. Do not let my past sins have a grip on me; rather, in your loving-kindness, please have mercy on me and use me however you want. Amen.

CHAPTER THREE

THE DIVINE MANDATE

"Then the eleven disciples went to Galilee, to the mountain where Jesus had told them to go. When they saw him, they worshiped him; but some doubted. Then Jesus came to them and said, 'All authority in heaven and on earth has been given to me. Therefore go and make disciples of all nations, baptizing them in the name of the Father and of the Son and of the Holy Spirit, and teaching them to obey everything I have commanded you. And surely I am with you always, to the very end of the age." Matthew 28:16-20

To run a successful ministry, God made me understand that I needed a specific message that would guide the ministry's operation. This message would ensure that the activities that happened on social media did not distract me. God also clearly gave me a message on which my ministry was to operate on.

It was on November 15, 2020, that the message came to me in a dream. God came in the form of my mentor, Apostle Belema Abili, and re-emphasized that He needed me to hold on to His calling. He said that He was the salt of the earth which could not lose its taste, and that as salt makes food tasteful for the eating, so I would make the lives of many worth living through the prophetic declarations which He would use me to make. He gave me the name 'Prophetess Rejoice' and the mandate to preach the message of salvation and deliverance to people online. This mandate has been the bedrock of my ministry. God truly empowered me with boldness and authority so that I would not get discouraged along the way.

In so many ways, God has shown His mighty works in my life and ministry. He has constantly placed spiritual helpers along my path. When I answered the call, He also revealed to me that he had attached three angels to work with me in my ministry. The names of my angels revealed to me were Archangel Gabriel, Angel Raphael, whose name means 'God heals', and the third was a lady fire angel, but her name was not revealed.

The presence of these angels has been evident in my life and ministry. They have strictly reminded me time and time again that I am the mouthpiece of God alone, and not of man. With the power of God in me, I have been able to perform healing, deliverance, and prophetic ministrations to all who tune in to listen to my ministrations. I return all the glory to God, and do not take the credit for myself.

If there is anything you should take from my story, is to please avoid procrastination as much as you can. Imagine all the spiritual and physical gifts and blessings that I missed just because I ignored God's call. There is nothing as fulfilling as letting God use you. He stirs up in your heart an hunger to do more for Him. Now, I feel so incomplete when I am not declaring His Kingdom on Facebook and winning more souls to Him.

My mind is continually renewed by His words as written in the Holy Bible. Every time I study God's Word or pray, the Holy Spirit keeps revealing hidden things to me. Deep truths are being laid bare to me, and I am gaining more understanding of how things work both in the physical and spiritual realm. To be honest, one of my fervent prayer points when I initially answered the call, even until now, has been that the Holy Spirit would help me in carrying out God's call to the end. The Holy Spirit has not failed me in this regard. Every time I study the scripture or have my private prayers, new insights are being released to me that are usually very instrumental in my being a useful vessel to God.

Some Christians make the mistake of not developing a healthy Bible study routine. As a true believer, the Word of God should constantly be found on your lips. How can you claim to have God's Word on your lips if you do not study it regularly and as Joshua 1:8 KJV admonishes us, to meditate on it day and night?

This book of the law shall not depart out of thy mouth; but thou shalt meditate therein day and night, that thou mayest observe to do according to all that is written therein: for then thou shalt make thy way prosperous, and then thou shalt have good success."

I have also learned to totally obey God in all things. There are times the Holy Spirit would reveal names for me to prophesy into their lives when I am on Facebook live ministrations. During these ministrations, just when I am about prophesying, the Holy Spirit would again instruct me not to go ahead with it, and I always obey completely without questioning.

These promptings by the Spirit of God are a way of testing our obedience to God. And if we fail to pass the test, He departs from us, and we become lost. Some believers fail to identify this test and, as such, allow their flesh to rule their understanding.

Another vital virtue I have discovered that pleases the Lord is total obedience to His instructions in our service to God. When God finds us to be obedient, He reveals even more hidden truths to us. Let us learn to imbibe this virtue so that God will be pleased to guide and bless us even more.

A PRAYER FOR YOU

Say this prayer: *Dear God, help me obey you completely. Help me understand that my wisdom is folly before you. Help me to meditate on your word day by day so that the truth of your Kingdom will be laid bare to me. Amen.*

CHAPTER FOUR

PROCRASTINATION AND DOUBT: THE TWO KILLERS OF DESTINY

Then I heard the Lord asking, "Whom should I send as a messenger to this people? Who will go for us? I said, "Here I am. Send me." Isaiah 6:8 (NLT)

There was more to God's question in *Isaiah 6:8* when He asked, *"Whom should I send as a messenger to this people?* You see, when God asked this question, He was not just looking for who would deliver His message. He was, in fact, looking for someone who was ready to give up their time to His service; someone who would obey Him completely in all things; someone who was not attached to the cares of this world; someone who could totally surrender their will to Him without a second thought.

This was the reason behind my initial hesitation. I was afraid that I would not have enough time to put into His service, given the mandate that the ministry He called me to was based on. I also thought about the resources needed to run an online ministry efficiently. I understood that I would constantly be doing Facebook live ministrations, but I was not sure I could afford the heavy data subscription bills. Then, I thought of the microphone needed to magnify my voice, the ring light for an extra brightening effect, and other equipment that would be required to run the ministry smoothly. I was also worried and scared that people would not even listen to my messages.

However, God made me understand that these things were not important to Him, and that what mattered most was the message of His Kingdom which He needed me to preach to the world. Remember what He said in the Gospel of *Matthew 6:33 (NKJV)*, *But seek first the Kingdom of God and His righteousness, and all these things shall be added to you.*

These words became evident in my ministry once I focused on getting the messages of Christ out to as many people as I could. He stirred up the hearts of people who donated generously to the growth of Rejoice E. Ministries. Now, I do not worry about the material things that my ministry needs. All I focus on is staying relevant in the hands of God for the work which He has called me to do. I try as much as I can to stay away from every appearance of evil because there is nothing as bad as the presence of God departing from you because of the sins you made the choice of committing.

"For God is light, in Him, there is no darkness at all" (1 John 1:5b). As a believer who is ready to be used by God - and I am not talking about being used in ministry alone, but in other aspects of life, the first thing you need do is to make yourself available, believing that every step of the way, He is there to direct you on what to do. Many times, we hear the voice of God calling us for His purpose, but we let doubt seize our hearts. We begin to ask in our subconscious: *"could it be that I really heard God call me? Is my mind playing tricks on me? If He really did, what are His plans for me? Is it something that I will figure out on my own? Am I fit to undertake this task?"*

Listen, when you let all these doubts cloud your mind, you become even more confused than before. Whereas all you need to do is to trust God completely and the words He spoke concerning you. Do not doubt Him; instead, trust Him with all of your heart. I love how the King James Version of the Bible interprets the words in the book of *Proverbs 3:5-6; it says, Trust in the Lord with all thine heart; and lean not unto thine own understanding. In all thy ways acknowledge him, and he shall direct thy paths.*

The next time you are tempted to doubt God's ability, please do not forget what I have shared with you. It is my earnest prayer that as you obey Him, you will be met with unmerited favors in whatever you set out to do.

A PRAYER FOR YOU

Say this prayer: Heavenly Father, I surrender myself to be used by you. Take my will and transform it into your own. Help me to trust completely in you, and do not let my human inclinations come in the way of your plans for me. Amen.

CHAPTER FIVE

LISTENING AS A KEY SPIRITUAL DISCERNMENT

"Call unto me, and I will answer thee, and show thee
great and mighty things, which thou knowest not."
Jeremiah 33:3 (KJV)

If you are well versed in matters of the Spirit, you will understand that it is important to also listen to what God has to say whenever we pray. Many Christians are always more concerned with just praying without listening. Prayer is a conversation between you and God. You talk, God listens, then God talks, and you listen. However, we often fall victim to not listening to God's side of the conversation. How do you hope to hear from God when you obviously do not listen to Him?

Why are you more concerned about telling God what bothers you without caring to hear Him tell you how to fix it? Or do you think God is dumb and cannot speak to you? Even if He spoke to you using someone else, you would still not recognize it because you have not developed that aspect of spiritual discernment.

If God had not opened my mind to understand some spiritual truths early, I might also have fallen short of having discernment. Most of the messages God has given to me have either been in the place of prayer or in study of His Word. Just imagine how lost I would be if I had not learned to listen to God during prayers and study time. I do not even want to think about the repercussions of being spiritually deaf as a believer.

In the early days of my ministry, God gave me some books of the Bible to study. These books talked about the prophetic as well as about false doctrines. Some of these books were Ezekiel, Revelations, and Jude. We live in a world filled with many spiritual beliefs; therefore, it is very common for Christians, especially those not firmly rooted in the Word of God, to get easily swayed by wolves in sheep's clothing, as the Bible calls them. There are many false prophets in this day and age that claim to preach the message of Christ; however, their sole purpose is to lure unsuspecting believers away from the Body of Christ. The Bible even warns us in *Matthew 7:15(NIV),"Watch out for false prophets. They come to you in sheep's clothing, but inwardly they are ferocious wolves.*

One good way of spotting these false prophets is by

having spiritual discernment. The good news is that we can each have spiritual discernment with the help of the Holy Spirit through a deep study of God's Word and prayers. Even with these activities, you also need to develop the act of listening because there is no way you can discern the Spirit if you do not listen carefully to what the Spirit of God has to say. This is the reason why listening is an essential part of prayer as well as a key careful study of His Word.

The devil is very much interested in luring as many people as He can to his Kingdom by getting them to be uninterested in the things of God. Considering the progressive advancements in technology and the access that it provides, sadly, many people, even Christians, relegate God to the background.

We now find it easier to sit before the TV screen and watch our favorite channels or series for hours. Even worse, we are comfortable on our cellphones practically all day and totally forget to eat, stretch, walk around, or do something productive. However, when it comes to studying God's Word or doing things that will boost our relationship with God, we find ourselves drifting off to sleep.

Many Christians who are not 'born again' find Sunday service boring for many reasons, for example, because there may be no 'upbeat music' like the secular world they are used to. Therefore, they fall victim to the teachings of false prophets, who make them believe that a bit of secularism can be borrowed into the worship of God.

So, you see a war waging where the Kingdom of darkness is trying to drown the Kingdom of God. We thank God for the gift of His Son Jesus Christ, who paid the ultimate price with His precious blood, so that we might be redeemed from the shackles of the Kingdom of darkness. *In him we have redemption through his blood, the forgiveness of sins, in accordance with the riches of God's grace. EPHESIANS 1:7 (NIV):*

The only times you find that lukewarm Christians remember God are when they are faced with challenges beyond their abilities to handle. They immediately return to God for help in fixing their problems. To this set of people, God is only a problem solver, and as such, they come to Him only when there is one. However, this is not the way it should be. You should have a personal relationship with God – one that goes beyond selfishness and religion. Once you have achieved this, it will be difficult to be swayed by false doctrines because you have a personal conviction of the awesomeness of God, as well as a discerning ear to hear Him speak to you.

It is for this reason that God called me to be His servant - to bring back those who have gone far from Him, especially those who have let the internet rule their minds and lives. I firmly believe that with God's help, His mandate over my ministry will be fulfilled; more souls will be won back to him, and His Kingdom will continue to reign supreme.

So, ask yourself today, *am I worshipping God for who He really is or for what I stand to gain from Him? Do I get carried away by what the rest of the world is doing or showcasing? Do I have a personal conviction of the greatness of God?* Asking yourself these personal questions will give you an idea of your standing with Christ, and show you whether you are on the right path or not. If we are honest, we know the areas of our relationship with God that we need to work on. I pray that you receive the anointing and grace to remain deeply rooted in the body of Christ. Amen.

A PRAYER FOR YOU

Say this prayer: *Lord Jesus, I thank you for the various channels you have given to us to communicate with you. Sweet Holy Spirit, please give me the ability to listen and hear God speak to me. Please grant me the Spirit of discernment so that I do not fall for the teachings of false prophets. Amen.*

CHAPTER SIX

OVERCOMING BY THE POWER OF GOD AT WORK

"For everyone born of God overcomes the world. This is the victory that has overcome the world, even our faith."
1 John 5:4 (NIV).

"I have told you these things, so that in me you may have peace. In this world you will have trouble. But take heart! I have overcome the world." John 16:33 (NIV)

"But thanks be to God! He gives us the victory through our Lord Jesus Christ." 1 Corinthians 15:57 (NIV)

" No, in all these things we are more than conquerors through him who loved us." Romans 8:37 (NIV)

One of the toughest ministries to venture into is that of salvation. This is because you are literally snatching lost souls back to God, and the devil does not find this funny one bit. Therefore, ministers involved in winning souls back to God are constantly faced with countless challenges - both physically and spiritually. That is the reason you can find a man or woman of God on fire for God, winning souls to Him, and doing many wonderful things to advance the Kingdom of God in one moment, and in another moment, they suddenly go down in grace and anointing because of temptation. We really need to pray for ministers of the gospel because we do not know the battles they fight daily to keep the message of Christ alive.

I have had my fair share of temptations from the devil, and I thank God for His grace over my life and the excellent support system that He has given to me. At one point, the devil tried all that he could to disconnect me from my spiritual mother, Apostle Belema Abili, but with the help of God's Spirit dwelling in me and the intercession from friends like Prophetess Juliet and the Lioness Group, all the devil's plans came out futile.

You must always remember never to take the role of mentors and support groups in your life for granted, regardless of whether you are a minister or not. These people provide additional support for you to lean on, especially when you are weak in Spirit. These people are simply God in the form of men sent to help you when things get rough. They encourage, advise, and hold you accountable to ensure that you do not derail from your goals and purpose. My advice is straight forward: if you do not have a mentor or support group, it is time to prayerfully get one.

On January 3, 2021, I recall waking up with what felt like a migraine headache. I could not explain what triggered it. I was in so much pain that I had to consult with my physician. He suspected that it could be one of the symptoms of COVID-19, given the uncertain times that we were facing globally. All glory be to God because the devil failed woefully - again. I was healed of the headache, and no virus like COVID-19 was found in my body. Hallelujah! The Word of God in *Deuteronomy 28:7 (NLT)* holds true in my life: "*The Lord will conquer your enemies when they attack you. They will attack you from one direction, but they will scatter from you in seven!*

My testimonies are many, and if I were to recount all of them, this book would become too voluminous to read. The truth is, whenever I am bothered about something and pray about it, God gives me a confirmation, either through his Word or through some other sign around me. So, whenever I am worried, I draw strength from the words found in *Deuteronomy 31:6(NLT)*, *"So be strong and courageous! Do not be afraid and do not panic before them. For the Lord your God will personally go ahead of you. He will neither fail you nor abandon you."*

My joy is that these awesome works of God are not only seen in my life. Many people who have listened to my live ministrations on Facebook and other social media platforms usually come back to testify of the miracles they have received upon listening to my ministrations. I would like to share a recent one that a lady sent to me after being a part of the first-ever, 24- hour fasting held in my ministry. I had to post the testimony on my social media platform to strengthen the faith of others.

AN OVERCOMER'S TESTIMONY

Khien is a resident of Massachusetts. She had been taking an online exam repeatedly with no success. Ironically, she had helped many people pass the same exam but was unable to succeed when she took hers. Upon tuning onto the 6 p.m. prayers held on my Facebook live ministration on the day of the fasting, she recounted that the instruction I gave was that they place both hands on their heads. Then, the prophecy came about a lady who had had an arrow shot to her head to cause memory loss, but that God was releasing angels to replace every loss.

Khien said she could not explain what was happening to her at the time, but that her head started to heat up, and she instantly became teary. The following day, she listened to the repeat of the live broadcast while trying to fix herself a meal. She recounted hearing a voice telling her to retake the exams. At the same time, an opposing voice told her not to bother because she had repeatedly taken the exams and met with failure every time. She chose not to listen to that second voice and went ahead to retake the three-hour exam in obedience to God's voice. To the glory of God, the result came out successful. Hallelujah!

There are many testimonies like hers of people who did not believe they could receive healing and restoration by simply listening to a woman of God speak on social media. This goes on to show that God is not limited to the four walls of a church building. He is everywhere. He is the ever Omnipotent, Omniscient, and Omnipresent God! He is ever ready to come through for you, but only if you invite Him to.

A PRAYER FOR YOU

Say this prayer: *Eternal Father, I am grateful for the many times you rescued me from the snares of the devil. I am grateful for the helpers and intercessors you constantly send my way in times of difficulty. I thank you for your healing upon my life, especially in those times when I had lost all hope. Thank you, God, for loving me. Amen.*

CHAPTER SEVEN

ENCOUNTERS

"The Word became flesh and made his dwelling among us. We have seen his glory, the glory of the one and only Son, who came from the Father, full of grace and truth."
John 1:14 (NIV)

MY ENCOUNTER AT THE PARK

Some time ago, one beautiful evening, while I was taking a walk at the park with two of my three beautiful children, Seyram and Elikem (Senam was not with us at the time), I saw a beautiful light, straight out of Heaven. It was so breathtaking that I knew it was a sign from God. As I sat on the bench to rest for a bit, the light appeared again. All I did was to keep singing praises to God, for behold, the Lord our God had shown us His   Glory and His Greatness.

At first, I thought I was the only one seeing it, but one of my daughters cleared that thought when she shared that she saw the heavens open, and behold, she saw a staircase and thought Heaven was coming upon us. Oh! What lovely daughter of mine! - Oh! what amazing Father of ours!

My dear people of God, the Kingdom of God is at

hand, and its manifestation is visible for everyone to see. Just as it is written in *Habakkuk 2:14 (NKJV), For the earth will be filled With the knowledge of the glory of the Lord, As the waters cover the sea.*

I write this book and share my experiences as an encouragement to all those in the faith, to keep fighting the good fight of faith, and to those not yet in faith, to say 'yes' to Jesus. Never resist God's Spirit. Always let Him lead and guide you because He is able to guide you into all truth *(John 16:13).*

MY VISION OF THE LION OF THE TRIBE OF JUDAH

I had a dream on June 13, 2020. In that dream, I had come back from work and fallen asleep. While I was sleeping, I saw a God in the form of a Lion surrounded by fire. The Lion spoke, saying, "I am the Lion of the Tribe of Judah." He gave me a key, and on the keyholder was written, 'The Lion of Tribe of Judah'. Then He said, "tell them I am coming very soon, I am coming very soon."

On waking up, I had a confirmation when I went on

Facebook. God had spoken through one of His servants about the Lion of Tribe of Judah and He had also led me to go online afterwards. I got ready and went online, and that was how He visited me and started speaking through me with His powerful words in my mouth.

He spoke thus (unabridged):
GOD'S VOICE THROUGH ME (GOD SPOKE THROUGH MY MOUTH).

"I am coming like a fire; I will have no mercy for any foolishness. Those that refuse to speak about me, I will say, 'I do not know you!'

I am coming like a fire, and there is no time for foolishness. I want everyone to be serious. My Spirit is grieved at those who speak against my servants. I told you I live inside of Rejoice, so her ways will be foolish to many. I live inside of her. Do not grieve her; if you grieve her, I will deal with you.

I will have no mercy for foolishness. I deal with those who contend with my words; I deal with them mercilessly.

The same way I sent my son Jesus into the world, and the world denied and persecuted Him, is the same way I have sent great servants. I have recruited many of my soldiers, and they are among you. Some of them are angels in human form. They carry wings, and I empower them. They see like eagles. When they speak, they speak like thunder; they speak like Me.

Can you not sense that when Rejoice is speaking, that is my voice speaking? When she speaks, you always say, 'We hear a man's (masculine) voice'. That is Me speaking. I come to speak directly to you through her. When you hear a man's voice, know that I, God, am the one speaking. I am God! I am God!

I have many names; if I say, 'worship me', then worship me. There are many of you who still harbor doubt, many who are hardened in your hearts.

Many are selfish, desiring personal gain that only brings atrocities and destruction.

Ask yourself, 'how old am I now? For how many years have I been seeking personal gain? How much have I gained through my selfishness?'

I have given you freedom and liberty to live. All I want is for you to worship Me. I release many warrior angels among you; some of them call you on the phone, and you are rude to them. Some of my angels ask for favors, and you are rude to them - all because you seek only your personal gain.

I am the Lion of the Tribe of Judah! I am very close; I am very close! I am coming like a fire! This is a warning to the Church; it is a warning! Repent and turn away from your wickedness. If you humble yourself, laying your life down for Me, I will raise you up. However, if you raise yourself, expecting me to lift you up, I will bring you down.

I have seen the hearts of many of you; the reason why you fellowship with me is because of personal gain. Your fellowship with me has nothing to do with genuine repentance. Every day, you are drinking the anointed water and saying salvation prayers, but you go back to your old ways, as though nothing happened. I release angels among you to watch you closely. If you are called by my name, you must act like Me.

I am coming like a fire, with no mercy for foolishness! I am using my own (vessels) who make themselves available. I am using them mightily. Many of them are wounded. To them, I say, 'just know that I am your comforter.'

The Spirit of a lying tongue has been released on the earth and many minds have been poisoned thereby. Be mindful so that you do not fall victim to this Spirit. I am judging the earth for the lying Spirit that they are using against many of my children. Many of you are dying spiritually but you are just walking about, like living corpses.

I am releasing my judgment of vengeance because of the things that you do secretly, thinking that no one is seeing you. You come out and wipe your faces clean in pretense when in fact, you are dead.

My words are sharper than a two-edged sword, piercing through bones, marrows, soul, and Spirit. If you accepted me, you would accept my Word in the Bible, but you do not read the Bible, so you are not close to me – in fact, you are far away from me. You reject me when you reject my Word. Your heart is far away from me.

My Word says, 'What shall it profit a man, if he shall gain the whole world, and lose his own soul?' (Mark 8:36).

Search your hearts; search your surroundings; make everything perfect before me! I am warning my Church to be ready for me because I am coming like a fire.

No mercy for foolishness! You know the truth, but you go before men and lie. I am grieved because many of you lie too much. You lie, and if I say that I will strike you like Ananias and Sapphira, you think that you can get away with it because you have not seen it happen in your time. Many of you are dead altogether, you are dead already!

If you repent, I am a merciful God. I will be a merciful Father to you because I love you very much. I want the ones that have labored in my name to be ready. I am coming like a fire; I have labored for many of you, but you all lie.

Today I am talking about personal gain because this is what is killing many of you. Your motivation is yourself. You say, 'it is all about me! me! me!'. I want to be in front of everyone; I want my name to be mentioned. You lie! You lie in front of my servants; you have no fear of my servants, though they represent me.

I always say that if you are indeed called by my name, if you indeed represent me well, why is it that when I give you an assignment, you lie because of personal gain?

I have come to warn my Church because I love you. Repent! Again, I say, my words are sharper than a two-edged sword, and you see it. You see that it is sharp, but you still tempt me. You still mock me and lie.

Many of you are dead altogether. There is no time for foolishness. I am judging the earth, and I will be taking my own with me before I do. I will take my own right before your eyes.

I am God! I am not a man to lie. Men lie as easily as the water they drink. I created all things in my image. Stop your evil ways, repent genuinely, and follow me. Then, you will be granted true access to my Kingdom.

I show myself to Rejoice. The day before she woke up from the dream where I showed myself to her, she had said, 'Father, I do not want to do your work anymore. The work and the people you have sent me to are difficult; I cannot do it.' She cried, saying she could not do my work.

When you cry in the secret place, I hear it. She cried, saying she did not want to work for the Kingdom. After her cry, I came and revealed myself to her, showing her that I am the

Lion of the Tribe of Judah. I have mercy on those that diligently seek me with genuine hearts. I do not have time for foolishness!

I told you all to remain serious and work for me seriously. Yet you play, you joke, and you do not see me like a Lion. That is why so many of you are dead already. You are dead altogether.

Rejoice did say that this work was too hard, and that all the people that I send her to are making the job difficult. You see, I speak through her. You hear my voice through her, but you still doubt. I chose her to work for me, and I told her she would suffer for my work. I have given her a great spirit. I did say that her ministry would be comfortable but that she would suffer for my work.

I have made her to be brutal and fearless. I have given her multiple anointings. This is the reason I named her 'Rainbow'; she is a fire! Every color she represents has a meaning. She will act and function in different dimensions and anointing, but she will suffer for my work. I am using her mightily, that is why she is restless. She is restless! She is brutal!"

God also spoke about a follower of the ministry, (Mercy Ngoran):

"Mercy Ngoran - Mercy, my daughter; my faithful servant; do not cry. I know the work that you do! I know the work you do. My reward is with me. You see the way I talk to my great prophet; I grant you access to my Throne. You carry my anointing - a heavy anointing. Many will persecute you because they are envious of you. Those who go through great persecution because the enemy sees the greatness in them - these are mine. They are fearless and brutal; they are dangerous to the Kingdom of darkness. They receive arrows, for my sake.

Oh! I am in your midst always. I have come to let people know that I see all that they do. Continue working for me with a sincere heart, and your reward is with me," says the Lord. 'Thank you, Jesus, thank you, Holy one!' was my quiet response. God has spoken! Let those that have ears hear and offer genuine repentance.

THE FIRST ANNIVERSARY
OF REJOICE E. MINISTRIES

July of 2021 made it a year since I responded to God's call to begin a Facebook ministry. To mark the first anniversary of Rejoice E. Ministries on Facebook, an anniversary event was held online, which featured several testimonies of salvation, healing, and deliverance from people who had been blessed by their connection to the ministry. The story of how I came in contact with my mentor and spiritual mother, Apostle Belema Abili, was also shared in full, along with the testimony of how God called me in July of 2020, which I have shared in this book. Indeed, I marvel at what God has done in just a year of Rejoice E. Ministries' presence on Facebook. I owe all the glory to Him alone.

TESTIMONIES FROM OTHER MEMBERS OF THE MINISTRY

As a source of encouragement to anyone needing a miracle, please read a few more testimonies sent in by members of the ministry.

From Christian Ndudi

Please, I want to share my testimony here with you, and

with brothers and sisters. Yesterday was my first time of tuning into your Facebook live program. When you were praying and sharing the Word of God to us, I experienced a miracle my miracle. I had been having severe chest pain since 2018, and while you spoke, I believe the Word of God instantly healed me. I no longer have chest pain. I am relieved! I give thanks to God for my healing, and I thank Him for you (Prophetess Rejoice). I believe that you are truly a Woman of God. May the Almighty God bless you more. Amen!

From Alice Hinze

Prophetess Rejoice, Sunday Blessings to you! Your video this morning was so powerful! I have listened to it three times, and I always feel like listening to it. Thank you!

A Testimony of Dream Restoration and Deliverance (Anonymous)

Hello Prophetess, I am here to testify to the goodness of God. Anything God cannot do does not exist. You prayed for me on Friday regarding my not being able to recall my dreams. To the glory of God, when I dream, I am now able to recall them. I am so happy, and I praise God. Thank you, Father, for restoration and deliverance. You are worthy to be praised. Thank you, Prophetess, for obeying the calling of God. May God bless you mightily. Amen!

Another Testimony of Deliverance (Anonymous)

Woman of God, glory to the Most High; glory to Yahweh, for He deserves it. Yesterday, I was led to watch your Facebook Live broadcast, and you read Psalm 31 which spoke to me directly. I commented and said, "I love this chapter!" Just then, you started to prophesy. Wow! Out of the blue, you mentioned my name, and my heart skipped a beat. Then you said, *"Every strange wickedness in your life that is causing affliction, may it receive the power of the Holy Ghost and be destroyed into ashes. Every land of desolation, may it be fruitful. God is removing the wall."* This is so true, Woman of God, as I had asked God to remove the wall in front of me - the strange wickedness causing work rejection, sickness, and lack of money in my life and my family's. A serpent spirit had done all of these, putting a wall in front of us. When we lost everything, we returned to the village, but God Himself had told me that He would destroy the enemy. Hallelujah!

FINAL NOTES

My story is proof that God can use anyone He pleases to fulfill His purpose on earth. He does not look at our qualifications, status, intelligence, righteousness or what we consider to be an eligibility standard. God clearly shows that He does not call the justified but justifies the 'called.' This means that no matter how red like crimson your sins may be, once God calls you, He justifies you, and when He justifies you, He glorifies you. Isn't that an amazing experience to have, simply by answering God's call? I am certain it is!

I also know that many of you may have condemned yourselves, saying, "I am not worthy of God's love because of the magnitude of the sins I have committed." If you remember that Jesus Christ died for you to have you freed from the bondage of sin, you will understand the extent of God's love for you. The guilt you constantly feel is the devil's way of making you feel miserable and undeserving of God's mercy and love.

Dear friend, please do not let the devil sow that lie in your mind and heart. Do not give him control of the reins of your life. Take back your life from the devil, then entrust it into the safe and loving arms of our Father. He will never leave you alone or disappointed. He has always been there for me in my ups and downs, and He is waiting to come through for you too. All you need do is simply call upon Him today because that is all God wants from you to intervene in your situation and on your behalf. Please invite him into your life and heart, and He will make you who live again.

WORDS OF KNOWLEDGE

Prophetic quotes by Prophetess Rejoice

- The sacrifices you make by working for God will break the bonds of the evil one.

- Make the turn first so that Christ can make the move.

- The treasure of God is inside you; do not allow the devil to steal it.

- When you are filled with the Holy Spirit, fear disappears.

- Your desperation to know Christ must be guided so you will not fall into the hands of teachers of false doctrine.

- Men act in the flesh without knowing that God owns their soul.

- May we pass the test of our faith

- The valley ends when hope comes

- Abraham's faith led him to God's inheritance

- Plant a seed of faith and it will germinate in victory

ENGAGE YOURSELF IN PRAYER, USING THE APPROPRIATE POWERFUL SCRIPTURES

All Scripture quotations in this section are from the New International Version (NIV) of the Bible

FOR GRACE

- "Grace and peace be yours in abundance through the knowledge of God and of Jesus our Lord."
  2 Peter 1:2

- "And all are justified freely by his grace through the redemption that came by Christ Jesus."
  Romans 3:24

- "Through whom we have gained access by faith into this grace in which we now stand. And we boast in the hope of the glory of God." *Romans 5:2*

- " For it is by grace you have been saved, through faith—and this is not from yourselves, it is the gift of God—" *Ephesians 2:8*

- "But he gives us more grace. That is why Scripture

says: "God opposes the proud but shows favor to the humble."James 4:6

- "Let us then approach God's throne of grace with confidence, so that we may receive mercy and find grace to help us in our time of need." *Hebrews 4:16*

FOR WISDOM

- "If any of you lacks wisdom, you should ask God, who gives generously to all without finding fault, and it will be given to you. But when you ask, you must believe and not doubt, because the one who doubts is like a wave of the sea, blown and tossed by the wind. That person should not expect to receive anything from the Lord. Such a person is double-minded and unstable in all they do." *James 1:5-8*

- "My son, if you accept my words and store up my commands within you, turning your ear to wisdom and applying your heart to understanding — indeed,

72

if you call out for insight and cry aloud for understanding, and if you look for it as for silver and search for it as for hidden treasure, then you will understand the fear of the Lord and find the knowledge of God. For the Lord gives wisdom; from his mouth come knowledge and understanding." *Proverbs 2:1-6*

- "But the wisdom that comes from heaven is first of all pure; then peace-loving, considerate, submissive, full of mercy and good fruit, impartial and sincere." *James 3:17*

- "I, wisdom, dwell together with prudence; I possess knowledge and discretion... Listen to my instruction and be wise; do not disregard it. Blessed are those who listen to me, watching daily at my doors, waiting at my doorway."
  Proverbs 8:12, 33-34

- "I have not stopped giving thanks for you,

remembering you in my prayers. I keep asking that the God of our Lord Jesus Christ, the glorious Father, may give you the Spirit of wisdom and revelation, so that you may know him better. I pray that the eyes of your heart may be enlightened in order that you may know the hope to which he has called you, the riches of his glorious inheritance in his holy people." *Ephesians 1:16-18*

FOR THE SPIRIT OF INTERCESSION

- "And pray in the Spirit on all occasions with all kinds of prayers and requests. With this in mind, be alert always keep on praying for all the Lord's people." *Ephesians 6:18*

- "Therefore I tell you, whatever you ask for in prayer, believe that you have received it, and it will be yours." *Mark 11:24*

- "Rejoice always, pray continually, give thanks in all circumstances; for this is God's will for you in Christ

Jesus. Do not quench the Spirit."

1 Thessalonians 5:16-19

- "Do not be anxious about anything, but in every situation, by prayer and petition, with thanksgiving, present your requests to God. And the peace of God, which transcends all understanding, will guard your hearts and your minds in Christ Jesus."

  Philippians 4:6-7

- "Therefore confess your sins to each other and pray for each other so that you may be healed. The prayer of a righteous person is powerful and effective."

  James 5:16

- "This is the confidence we have in approaching God: that if we ask anything according to his will, he hears us. And if we know that he hears us—whatever we ask—we know that we have what we asked of him." *1 John 5:14-1*

- "If you remain in me and my words remain in you, ask whatever you wish, and it will be done for you." *John 15:7*

- "Jesus replied, 'Truly I tell you, if you have faith and do not doubt, not only can you do what was done to the fig tree, but also you can say to this mountain, 'Go, throw yourself into the sea,' and it will be done. If you believe, you will receive whatever you ask for in prayer." *Matthew 21:21-22*

- "This, then, is how you should pray: 'Our Father in heaven, hallowed be your name, your Kingdom come, your will be done, on earth as it is in heaven. Give us today our daily bread. And forgive us our debts, as we also have forgiven our debtors. And lead us not into temptation, but deliver us from the evil one." *Matthew 6:9-13*

- "So I say to you: Ask and it will be given to you; seek and you will find; knock and the door will be opened to you." *Luke 11:9*

- "Call to me and I will answer you and tell you great and unsearchable things you do not know." *Jeremiah 33:3*

- "Whoever dwells in the shelter of the Most High will rest in the shadow of the Almighty. I will say of the Lord, "He is my refuge and my fortress, my God, in whom I trust." Surely he will save you from the fowler's snare and from the deadly pestilence. He will cover you with his feathers, and under his wings you will find refuge; his faithfulness will be your shield and rampart." *Psalm 91:1-4*

- "In the same way, the Spirit helps us in our weakness. We do not know what we ought to pray for, but the Spirit himself intercedes for us through wordless groans." *Romans 8:26*

- "The smoke of the incense, together with the prayers

of God's people, went up before God from the angel's hand." *Revelations 8:4*

FOR SPIRITUAL STRENGTH, ESPECIALLY IN TIMES OF TROUBLE

- "God is our refuge and strength, an ever-present help in trouble. Therefore we will not fear, though the earth give way and the mountains fall into the heart of the sea, though its waters roar and foam and the mountains quake with their surging." *Psalm 46:1-3*

- "The name of the Lord is a fortified tower; the righteous run to it and are safe." *Proverbs 18:10*

- "Nehemiah said, 'Go and enjoy choice food and sweet drinks, and send some to those who have nothing prepared. This day is holy to our Lord. Do not grieve, for the joy of the Lord is your strength." *Nehemiah 8:10*

- "So do not fear, for I am with you; do not be dismayed, for I am your God. I will strengthen you and help you; I will uphold you with my righteous right hand." *Isaiah 41:10*

- "The Lord is my strength and my defense; he has become my salvation. He is my God, and I will praise him, my father's God, and I will exalt him." *Exodus 15:2*

- "The Lord is a refuge for the oppressed, a stronghold in times of trouble. Those who know your name trust in you, for you, Lord, have never forsaken those who seek you." *Psalm 9:9-10*

- "Look to the Lord and his strength; seek his face always." *1 Chronicles 16:11*

- "You are my hiding place; you will protect me from trouble and surround me with songs of deliverance. I will instruct you and teach you in the way you should go; I will counsel you with my loving eye on you." *Psalm 32:7-8*

- "The righteous cry out, and the Lord hears them; he delivers them from all their troubles." *Psalm 34:17*

- "But now, this is what the Lord says— he who created you, Jacob, he who formed you, Israel: 'Do not fear, for I have redeemed you; I have summoned you by name; you are mine. When you pass through the waters, I will be with you; and when you pass through the rivers, they will not sweep over you. When you walk through the fire, you will not be burned; the flames will not set you ablaze. For I am the Lord your God, the Holy One of Israel, your Savior; I give Egypt for your ransom, Cush and Sebain your stead." *Isaiah 43:1-3*

- "…and said to them, 'I know that the Lord has given you this land and that a great fear of you has fallen on us, so that all who live in this country are melting in fear because of you." *Joshua 2:9*

- "The Lord is near to all who call on him, to all who call on him in truth. He fulfills the desires of those who fear him; he hears their cry and saves them." *Psalm 145:18-19*

- "Surely God is my salvation; I will trust and not be afraid. The Lord, the Lord himself, is my strength and my defense; he has become my salvation." *Isaiah 12:2*

- "When I called, you answered me; you greatly emboldened me." *Psalm 138:3*

- "But he said to me, "My grace is sufficient for you, for my power is made perfect in weakness." Therefore I will boast all the more gladly about my weaknesses, so that Christ's power may rest on me." *2 Corinthians 12:9*

- "He gives strength to the weary and increases the power of the weak." *Isaiah 40:29*

FOR THE SPIRIT OF OBEDIENCE

- "Now if you obey me fully and keep my covenant, then out of all nations you will be my treasured possession." *Exodus 19:5A-6*

- "Love the Lord your God and keep His requirements, His decrees, His laws and His commands always." *Deuteronomy 11:1*

- "We demolish arguments and every pretension that sets itself up against the knowledge of God, and we take captive every thought to make it obedient to Christ." *2 Corinthians 10:5*

- "Children, obey your parents in the Lord, for this is right. "Honor your father and mother"—which is the first commandment with a promise— "so that it may go well with you and that you may enjoy long life on the earth." *Ephesians 6:1-3*

- "Have confidence in your leaders and submit to their authority, because they keep watch over you as those who must give an account." *Hebrews 13:17*

- "You are my friends if you do what I command." *John 15:14*

- "If you love me, keep my commands." *John 14:15*

- "He replied, "Blessed rather are those who hear the word of God and obey it." *Luke 11:28*

- "Slaves, obey your earthly masters in everything; and do it, not only when their eye is on you and to curry their favor, but with sincerity of heart and reverence for the Lord." *Colossians 3:22*

- "For just as through the disobedience of the one man the many were made sinners, so also through the obedience of the one man the many will be made righteous." *Romans 5:19*

- "As obedient children, do not conform to the evil desires you had when you lived in ignorance." *1 Peter 1:14*

FOR THE SPIRIT OF BOLDNESS AND COURAGE

- "The Lord is my light and my salvation— whom shall I fear? The Lord is the stronghold of my life— of whom shall I be afraid?" *Psalm 27:1*

- "But I will make you as unyielding and hardened as they are. I will make your forehead like the hardest stone, harder than flint. Do not be afraid of them or terrified by them, though they are a rebellious people." *Ezekiel 3:8-9*

- "Have I not commanded you? Be strong and courageous. Do not be afraid; do not be discouraged, for the Lord your God will be with you wherever you go." *Joshua 1:9*

- "For the Spirit God gave us does not make us timid, but gives us power, love and self-discipline." *2 Timothy 1:7*

- "...according to his eternal purpose that he accomplished in Christ Jesus our Lord. In him and through faith in him we may approach God with freedom and confidence."*Ephesians 3:11-12*

- "I pray that out of his glorious riches he may strengthen you with power through his Spirit in your inner being." *Ephesians 3:16*

- "Take the helmet of salvation and the sword of the Spirit, which is the word of God. And pray in the Spirit on all occasions with all kinds of prayers and requests. With this in mind, be alert and always keep on praying for all the Lord's people. Pray also for me, that whenever I speak, words may be given me so that I will fearlessly make known the mystery of the gospel." *Ephesians 6:17-19*

- "Keep your lives free from the love of money and be content with what you have, because God has said, 'Never will I leave you; never will I forsake you.' So we say with confidence, 'The Lord is my helper; I will not be afraid. What can mere mortals do to me?" *Hebrews 13:5-6*

- "And because of my chains, most of the brothers and sisters have become confident in the Lord and dare all the more to proclaim the gospel without fear." *Philippians 1:14*

- "I can do all this through him who gives me strength." *Philippians 4:13*

CONCLUSION

If you are reading this book and you know you are not born again, or are not sure that if you died today, you would make heaven, please say this SALVATION PRAYER:

Dear Lord Jesus, I know that I am a sinner, and I ask for your forgiveness. I believe you died for my sins and rose from the dead. I turn from my sins and invite you to come into my heart and life. I want to trust and follow you as my Lord and Savior, in Jesus' Name, I pray. *Amen.*

Congratulations to you, as you are now a member of the Body of Jesus Christ, our Savior.

May God bless you richly.

ABOUT THE AUTHOR

Prophetess Rejoice Esi Hlovor is the founder of the Rejoice E. Ministries, an online ministry with the mandate of preaching salvation and deliverance to the thousands of people who use Facebook every day. She first received the assignment of beginning an online ministry in June 2020 in a dream, and she heeded the call after ignoring it severally.

Rejoice was born and raised in Ghana in the Volta Region but later relocated and is now based in Dublin, Ireland. She studied marketing in Customer Service at Ibat college and Bio-Pharmaceutical at I T Sligo University and currently works as a care support worker.

She is blessed with three adorable children and is dedicated to raising them in the way of the Lord. Rejoice is a Prophetess and a motivational speaker, and through her online platforms and by the help of the Holy Spirit, she has been able to give hope to the downcast and preach the message of Christ to the many people who have come across her ministry. Her online ministry on Facebook, Rejoice Esi Ministry, has recorded numerous testimonies from people whose lives have been impacted and who her prophecies have delivered. She is blessed to have solid spiritual support in the persons of Apostle Paul Gidi Gasu, her spiritual Father, and Apostle Belema Abili, her mentor and spiritual mother. It is her dream that God will use her as His vessel to bring salvation and liberation to the many who will come in contact with her.

Notes

_____

_____

_____

_____

_____

_____

_____

_____

_____

_____

_____

_____

_____

_____

Notes

Notes

Notes

CPSIA information can be obtained
at www.ICGtesting.com
Printed in the USA
BVHW040944130122
626142BV00012B/291